SMYTHE GAMBRELL
LIBRARY

WESTMINSTER SCHOOLS

PRESENTED BY

Kenny Chastain

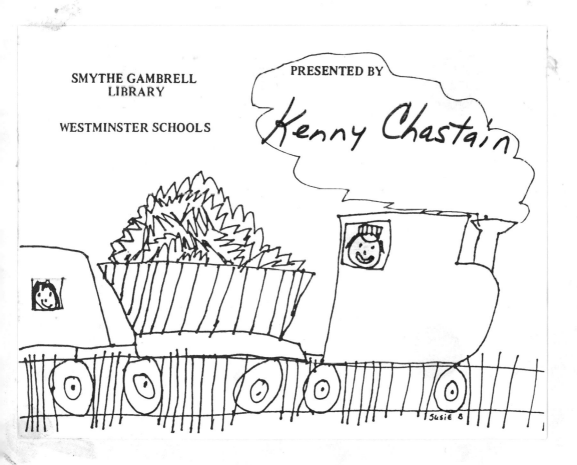

A Civilization Project Book

ANCIENT EGYPT

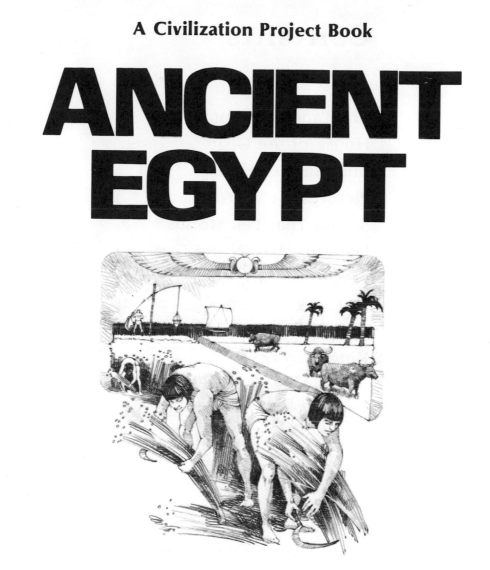

BY SUSAN PURDY
AND CASS R. SANDAK

Illustrations and diagrams by Beverly Pardee

Franklin Watts   New York/London/Toronto/Sydney   1982

Contents

The Land of Egypt   **3**

House of the Dead   **6**

Burying the Dead   **9**

Pictures for Words   **12**

Scrolls That Tell Stories   **13**

Hieroglyphics Name Cartouche   **14**

Frieze Paintings   **16**

A Jeweled Pectoral   **18**

Queen's Headdress   **20**

King's Crown   **22**

A Movable Crocodile   **23**

Senat: An Ancient Board Game   **26**

The Chariot: A War Machine   **28**

Index   **32**

Library of Congress Cataloging in Publication Data

Purdy, Susan Gold
  Ancient Egypt.

  (A Civilization project book)
  Includes index.
  Summary: Briefly traces the development of ancient Egyptian civilization and gives instructions for making models of such Egyptian artifacts as pyramids, hieroglyphics, papyrus scrolls, frieze paintings, board games, and jewelry.
  1. Egypt—Civilization—To 332 B.C.—Juvenile literature. 2. Handicraft—Egypt—Juvenile literature.
[1. Egypt—Civilization—To 332 B.C. 2. Handicraft.
3. Models and modelmaking] I. Sandak, Cass R.
II. Title. III. Series.
DT61.P87   932'.01   82-6962
ISBN 0-531-04452-1   AACR2

The Land of Egypt

Ancient Egypt was a narrow strip of land in the northeastern corner of Africa. It extended for several hundred miles through the valley of the river Nile. The Nile flows through the Sahara Desert, which stretches across North Africa. Here the climate is hot and dry.

In prehistoric times, Egypt was settled by hunters driven north from drought-stricken Central Africa. In the Nile Valley they turned to herding and agriculture.

In ancient times, Egypt was called "the gift of the Nile," because the strip of land was enriched by fertile soil that was deposited when the Nile overflowed its banks each summer between June and September. When the waters subsided, they left behind a layer of rich soil. Farmers started their growing seasons each autumn. During the period of drought from March to May, they harvested their crops of barley, wheat, grapes, vegetables, and fruits. Irrigation systems and efficient farming methods led to a flourishing economy.

In time, two separate kingdoms developed—Upper Egypt, consisting of the hills and highlands of southern Egypt, and Lower Egypt, including the plains of northern Egypt and the delta and mouth of the Nile. Around 3100 B.C., King Narmer of Upper Egypt conquered the kingdom of Lower Egypt. This made Egypt a unified country ruled by a single king, or Pharaoh.

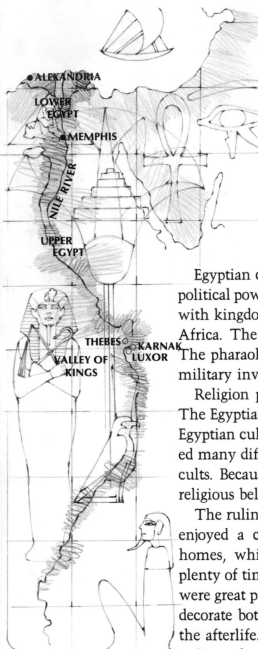

Principal sites of ancient Egypt

ALEXANDRIA

LOWER EGYPT

MEMPHIS

NILE RIVER

UPPER EGYPT

THEBES KARNAK
VALLEY OF LUXOR
KINGS

Egyptian civilization advanced. The pharaohs extended their political power through foreign conquest and international trade with kingdoms in the eastern end of the Mediterranean and in Africa. The Egyptians were capable boat builders and sailors. The pharaohs' armies helped to extend Egypt's influence with military inventions like the chariot.

Religion played an important role in ancient Egyptian life. The Egyptians worshiped a great number of gods and goddesses. Egyptian culture developed over a long period of time and united many different groups that had their own gods and religious cults. Because of this, the Egyptians had a rich assortment of religious beliefs and myths.

The ruling classes of nobles, priests, and government officials enjoyed a cultured and leisurely life centered around their homes, which were really self-supporting estates. They had plenty of time for feasting and relaxation. The wealthier classes were great patrons of the arts and hired painters and sculptors to decorate both their homes and their tombs, in preparation for the afterlife.

Since they left so much of themselves behind in their writings and works of art, the ancient Egyptians are well known to us today. They were great artists and architects. Massive structures—pyramids, sphinxes, temples, obelisks, and other monuments—adorned their cities and shrines and still dot the countryside of Egypt. Painters and sculptors followed a set of rigid stylistic rules that were in use from around 3400 B.C. Sculpture was massive and basically symmetrical; it showed little move-

ment or individual features. Still, Egyptian artists were sensitive and highly skilled. They have left artistic works that document the many aspects of their lives.

Gold jewelry inset with semiprecious stones and pieces of furniture fitted together from rare woods, ivory, and gold have been found in Egyptian tombs. Along with sculptures, mummies, and papyruses, they now fill museum galleries around the world and attest to the skill of Egyptian craftsmen.

Egyptian history is divided into a number of periods, based on the thirty different ruling families, or dynasties, of pharaohs who ruled between 3200 and 332 B.C.

In 322 B.C., Alexander the Great conquered Egypt and brought Greek civilization to the country. Alexander was so impressed with Egypt that he established his capital at Alexandria and set up the Ptolemaic Dynasty. Cleopatra was the last of the Ptolemies, and she ruled until 30 B.C., when the Romans conquered Egypt.

Civilization had already flourished in Egypt for more than 3,000 years when the Romans made Egypt one of their provinces. Both the Greeks and the Romans learned much from the ancient Egyptians and brought many of their ideas and inventions to Europe where they helped to shape the modern world.

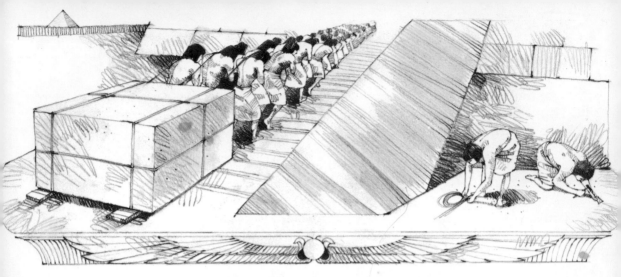

House of the Dead

A pyramid is a house of the dead, a tomb for the Pharaoh and his family. It consists of an underground burial chamber topped by a monument, usually built from huge blocks of limestone. The stone blocks were cut by copper chisels and mallets or hand-held stone picks. A series of holes were cut in a line on the stone. Then workers drove wooden wedges into the holes to split the stone. Stones were moved by barge up the Nile. Once on land, the stone blocks were placed on sledges. Slaves hauled the sledges over wooden rollers by pulling on towropes made of papyrus. Water was poured in front of the rollers as a lubricant. The stones were towed on the sledges up the sides of the pyramid on ramps of sand. Then the blocks were levered into place. When the pyramid was finished, workers dug away the sand.

The Great Pyramid of Cheops was built at Giza around 2600 B.C. Its base is a square 755 feet (230 m) on each side. The base covers 13 acres (5.2 hectares) of land. The pyramid rises to a height of 482 feet (144.5 m) in over two hundred stepped tiers. Almost 2,500,000 blocks of stone were used, each block weighing from 2½ to 70 tons. After the stepped pyramid was built at Giza, it was faced with smooth polished blocks, most of which have been carried away over the years for use in other buildings. Our paper model is based on this design.

Materials you will need:

Sheet of oaktag, construction paper, or other stiff paper about 20 inches (50 cm) square, pencil, felt-tip pen, ruler, right-angle ruler, scissors, glue, cardboard, sand (optional) or sand-colored paint

A. 1. In the middle of the stiff paper, draw a square 7½ inches (19 cm) on each side.

2. Divide each side of the square in half and draw lines (as shown in Figure 1) that extend 6 inches (15 cm) out from the midpoints on the sides as shown. Mark these points A, B, C, and D.

3. Draw lines from each point to the corners of the square closest to it (dotted lines, Figure 2). This will make four triangles with sides of equal length.

4. Draw two fastening tabs on the triangles that are opposite each other as shown in Figure 2. Each tab should be about 1 inch (2.5 cm) wide and 2 inches (5 cm) long. Draw the tabs roughly on the middle of each side.

5. Draw diagonal lines connecting the opposite corners of the base square.

6. Label each triangle as shown (1,2,3,4).

B. To see inside the pharaoh's burial chamber, make an interior view panel.

1. Draw a triangle as shown in Figure 3. Mark a base line 10½ inches (26.5 cm) long on the paper's edge.

2. Divide the base line in half, marking a point 5¼ inches (13 cm) in from the edge. Use the right-angle ruler to mark a top line 4¾ inches (12 cm) above the center point. Connect the top point and the edges of the base line.

3. Draw tabs A and B the same size as the pyramid tabs. Add tab C.

4. Cut the shape out around the heavy black line as shown in Figure 3.

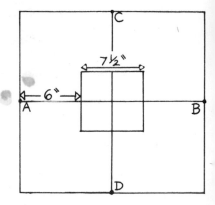

Figure 1

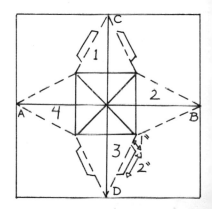

Figure 2

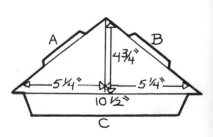

Figure 3

7

C. On this panel, draw a diagram of the pyramid's interior and label the parts as shown in Figure 4.

1. Fold back tabs A and B.

2. Fold tab C forward.

3. Fold the pyramid tabs over onto the front of each triangle.

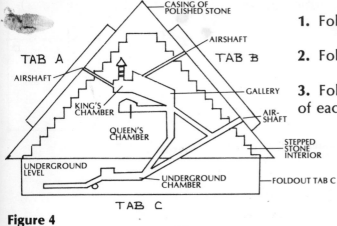

Figure 4

D. The interior panel will now fit inside the pyramid.

1. Spread glue on the underside of folded-out tab C.

2. With this tab forward, glue the base line onto the diagonal line as shown in Figure 5.

3. Then glue the side tabs of the interior panel onto triangles 1 and 4 using the tabs to hold them together.

4. Fold triangles 2 and 3 toward the inside. If you want to close the pyramid entirely, put a piece of double-sided tape on each tab of triangle 3. Press it against sides 2 and 4 to close them up, or leave sides 2 and 3 open so you can view the interior.

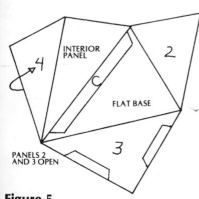
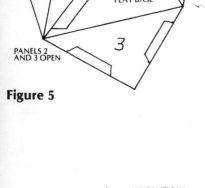

Figure 5

E. You can make a base for your pyramid.

1. Cut a 12-inch (30.5-cm) square of stiff cardboard.

2. Spread it with glue and sprinkle on a coating of sand. Shake off any loose sand. Or, paint the board to look like sand.

3. To attach the pyramid, spread glue on the bottom of the pyramid base and press it down on the platform. (See Figure 6.)

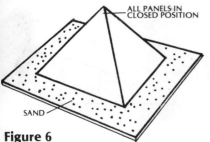

Figure 6

Burying the Dead

The ancient Egyptians believed in life after death. Because of this, it was important for the dead body to be well preserved and to remain as complete as possible, so that the soul could return to it and live in it forever. Embalmers used elaborate methods to mummify, or preserve, the body. First, the brain was drawn out through the nose with a wire hook. The heart, the liver, and other internal organs were removed through a cut in the abdomen. They were set aside and preserved in special *canopic* jars. Then the body was covered with a salt called *natron*, to remove moisture. The body was then washed and rubbed with sweet-smelling oils. The inside of the body, where the organs had been, was packed with linen. At last, the body was wrapped with layers of linen strips. The entire process of mummification took about seventy days. The completed mummy was placed inside one or more coffins, or mummy cases. The Egyptians mummified not only people, but sacred animals like cats, crocodiles and beetles.

You can make a model of a mummy and mummy case out of papier-mâché. The model can be small, or life-size, depending upon the amount of time you wish to spend on the project. A life-size mummy would be a good project for an entire class or group to work on together.

Materials you will need:
Old newspapers, glue or wallpaper paste, bucket, water, aluminum foil, masking tape, wire mesh (for life-size mummy), spool wire and wire cutters, tempera paints, rolls of white cotton strips or gauze bandages, beige or tan cloth or packing tape, scissors, pencil

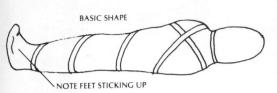

BASIC SHAPE

NOTE FEET STICKING UP

Figure 1

A. 1. Make your mummy any size you like. To make a small mummy, crumple newspaper into a basic body form. Wrap it with tape to hold the shape (see Figure 1). For a life-size model, bend wire mesh to form the basic shape and hold it in place with tape or spool wire.

2. After the basic form is made, follow the boxed instructions to prepare a papier-mâché mixture. Tear strips of newspaper and dip them into the mixture.

3. Put layers of the wet strips over the basic form to make the shape firm. Then take strips of cotton or gauze bandages and dip them into the glue. Wrap these strips around the body until it is entirely bound. If the figure gets too soggy, let it dry out before applying more layers of papier-mâché.

Figure 2

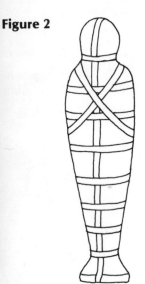

4. Let the papier-mâché dry thoroughly (probably overnight). Finally, bind the whole figure with brown or beige cloth or tape into the pattern shown (see Figure 2).

B. 1. To make a case for your mummy, make a mold of its shape and size by wrapping the model mummy in foil.

2. Slide the mummy out of the foil carefully so that the shape is retained. Stuff the inside of the foil with crumpled newspaper to hold the shape of the model mummy. Tape the foil closed.

3. Cover the foil shape with papier-mâché, building up thick layers that are smooth on the outside.

4. When the papier-mâché has dried, paint a face and hair on the outside (Figure 3).

> **PAPIER-MÂCHÉ MIX** Use either white glue or wallpaper paste mixture. If using white glue, mix 2/3 part glue with 1/3 part water to make a creamy mixture. Wallpaper paste is usually mixed 1 part powder to 10 parts water (but follow the directions on the box). Sometimes you may need to add more powder to get a slightly thicker mixture.

Figure 3

C. 1. For a life-size mummy, wrap the completed mummy with wire mesh to make a mold of its size and shape. Remove the mummy carefully and wire the mesh together to hold.

2. Use wire cutters to cut the form lengthwise in half. Tape the cuts closed. This will make it easier to open.

3. Cover the mesh with layers of papier-mâché until you have built up sturdy sides that are smooth and even and conform to the basic mummy shape.

4. Build up a face and hair as shown (Figure 4).

5. Let the case dry thoroughly.

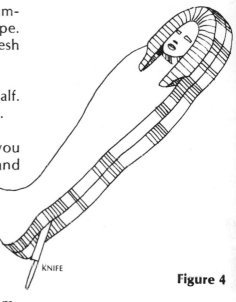

KNIFE

Figure 4

D. 1. When the papier-mâché is thoroughly dry, complete the small model by using a knife or scissors to cut the case in half lengthwise (Figure 4). For a life-size mummy, you can cut the papier-mâché case in half lengthwise and lift it off the wire mesh. Or, more easily, cut the papier-mâché with a knife, and then use wire cutters to cut the tape holding the two halves of the mesh together. Lift the two halves apart, keeping the papier-mâché and the mesh as one unit. With scissors or sandpaper, smooth any rough edges. Bend any sharp wire ends under.

2. Fit the mummy inside its case to test the size. It should fit easily, but without too much extra space.

3. Remove the mummy.

4. Paint the outside and inside of the case with gold or white acrylic or poster paints.

5. Decorate the case with colorful scenes of the person mummified. Or, use hieroglyphic symbols and the person's name in a cartouche (see pages 14 and 15). Paint a stylized face and a wide beaded collar, following the traditional rules of Egyptian painting (see pages 16 and 17). Paint a funereal pendant of "Ba," the soul-bird, on the case (see pages 18 and 19), or follow Figure 5 for ideas.

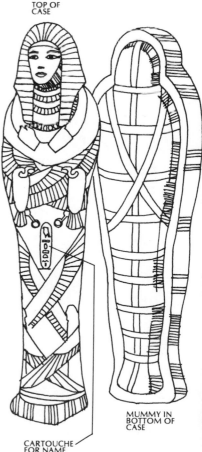

TOP OF CASE

MUMMY IN BOTTOM OF CASE

CARTOUCHE FOR NAME

Figure 5

11

Pictures for Words

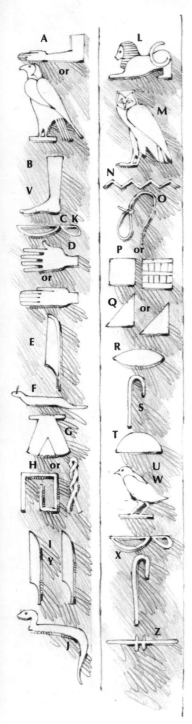

Hieroglyphics is a form of writing that uses pictures to convey ideas. For example, the picture of a stringed musical instrument stands for the words pleasure, joy, and goodness [♃]. Every hieroglyphic figure, or "character," is a picture of an object. The signs can be used singly in a line to tell a story, or they can be grouped, to make words based on the meanings of the groups of pictures. The symbol for "god" plus "woman" means "goddess," making a combined picture word.

Later, the characters came to stand for sounds. The first letter of the name of an object was given to the picture that represented it. Then that character stood for that sound, or phonetic value. The phonetic alphabet developed from the need for simplified writing.

Hieroglyphics are written in columns or horizontal lines. They are read from left to right or from right to left, depending upon which way the people, birds, and animals face in the particular writing you see. You read *toward* these characters.

To show plurals, pictures were followed by three dots in a horizontal or vertical line, or three lines. Occasionally the sign itself was repeated three times.

Sometimes hieroglyphic characters were painted, sometimes they were cut in stone or wood, in relief or intaglio, or written with a reed and dye on papyrus.

1. Study the hieroglyphics shown and their meanings. Make up a list of your own ideas for picture writing, designing nouns and verbs with simple shapes that are easy to understand. Follow the rules for making plurals. Write in horizontal or vertical lines.

2. Make up a simple story and write it in your scroll (see pages 13 and 14) using either the traditional hieroglyphics or your own designs. If you like, you can also write a translation alongside the pictographs.

Scrolls That Tell Stories

A group of educated officials in ancient Egypt was called *scribes*. They copied religious texts and kept records on scrolls. These were made from papyrus, a kind of paper made from the stalk of the papyrus plant. The English word paper comes from the name papyrus. The Egyptians learned to make paper from papyrus during the First Dynasty, around 3100 B.C. Written language dates roughly from this time, although the idea had developed earlier elsewhere.

The Egyptians wrote on the papyrus with a reed about 10 inches (25 cm) long and 1/8 inch (0.3 cm) in diameter. The end of the reed was crushed to make a flexible brush; it was not cut into a sharpened point. Vegetable dye or colored earth was mixed with vegetable gum and water to make an ink for writing.

To show the ancient Egyptian method of making paper accurately, genuine papyrus would be needed. Because this plant is rare in most parts of the modern world, we will make our scroll with ordinary paper. However, you can use a reed brush and natural dye ink to write on the scroll.

Materials you will need:
Several sheets of lightweight paper such as typing paper, glue or clear tape, two wooden dowels or sticks, tacks or staples, a reed for writing, a hammer or mallet, purple berry juice or boiled walnut bark, ribbon

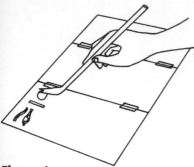

Figure 1

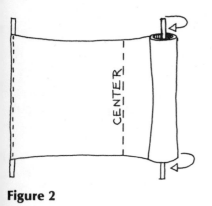

Figure 2

1. Use transparent tape or glue to fasten several sheets of paper together (typing paper size or slightly larger), side by side to make a long strip (see Figure 1).

2. To make a brush for writing, use a reed or a thin stick. Crush the tip with a hammer or mallet to make a brush. Dip the brush into ink, berry juice, or walnut bark boiled with water to make a brown dye. Draw hieroglyphic symbols on your papyrus sheet and/or paint Egyptian style pictures on the scroll (see page 12).

3. Tack or staple each end of the paper strip to a wooden pole that is slightly longer than the paper. Roll the scroll inward toward the middle, rolling half the paper on each pole. Tie the scroll together with a strip of ribbon, as in Figure 2.

Hieroglyphics Name Cartouche

Ancient Egyptians believed that a cartouche hanging around their necks acted as a magic amulet to ward off injury or the evil eye. A cartouche is an oval or oblong design showing a person's name, the way we might use a monogram or emblem. In tablets of hieroglyphics, the names of kings, queens, and gods always appear with a cartouche placed either vertically or horizontally. The cartouche shape itself—the outline of the oblong with a line at one end—is the hieroglyphic sign for "name."

You can make your own name cartouche out of a plaster of Paris shape marked with the hieroglyphics representing the phonetic sounds of your name. To identify which hieroglyphic sign goes with which English letter, look at the alphabet table on page 12. You will notice that in some cases, there is more than one way to depict a single sound. Also, the ancient Egyptian language used some sounds that we do not. These have been omitted.

Materials you will need:
Plaster of Paris, bucket, water, flat surface covered with wax paper, sandpaper, emery board, thick darning needle or toothpick, gold or black paint, sharply pointed needle, string or shoelace, pinback, glue

1. In the bucket, mix plaster of Paris with water to make a thick, pudding-like mixture. You may need to let the mixture sit a few minutes to thicken sufficiently. Stir the mixture to be sure it is free of lumps.

2. Use your hands to shape ovals on the wax paper. The ovals should be about the length of your little finger (see Figure 1). They should be about the width of two of the knuckles on that finger and about ¼ inch (.5 cm) thick. Make a hole for hanging in one end (or later, glue a pin on the back).

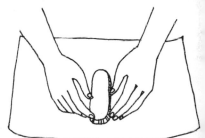

Figure 1

3. Let the shapes harden thoroughly. Pick the shapes off the wax paper and sand or file smooth on the front and edges. Drill your hanging hole open with the point of the needle, as in Figure 2.

4. Paint the front with gold or black paint and let it dry.

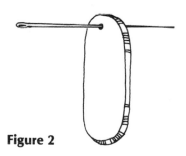

Figure 2

5. On scrap paper, copy the hieroglyphics that make up the sounds (not the actual spelling) in your name. Omit any silent letters. After you decide on the symbols, copy them on your cartouche by scratching them into the painted surface with the point of the needle (see Figure 3). The white plaster will show through the lines. Blow off the scratched plaster dust.

6. Tie a hanging string through the hole and wear the cartouche around your neck. If you wish, glue a pin on the back side.

Figure 3

Frieze Paintings

Egyptian artists decorated the walls of their temples and tombs with paintings of religious subjects and views of daily life. Instead of showing realistic views, the paintings conveyed ideas. To create these ideas, artists developed and followed certain conventions, or rules.

The order and arrangement of the scene was very important. The viewer should be able to "read" or understand the picture immediately. To show his importance, the king or ruler was always the largest figure. Women, common people, and servants were always smaller.

A figure in an Egyptian painting is shown with the head in profile. The eyes (usually one eye) are shown as they look from the front, but they have no particular expression. The eyebrows are ribbon-like. This style creates a mask-like look—the way one wished to look in the next life—rather than a specific portrait. The shoulders and torso are sometimes shown in profile, but usually a frontal view is used so that this part of the body can be completely and easily understood in its most characteristic form. The legs and feet are shown in profile because this is the most easily recognized view of these limbs.

Animals, fish, and birds were shown in profile for ease in identification. To show objects in depth, they were overlapped in layers. Perspective was not used.

The figures were painted first in outline, then filled in with areas of solid flat colors. Men were usually shown with a darker skin tone than women. Animals and plants were painted with earth tones of terra-cotta, red, yellow,

green, brown, and white. Shades of blue were used for sky and water and sometimes for highlighting the figures. No shading or indication of light and dark was used.

The purpose of Egyptian tomb painting was not purely decorative. Like all artifacts buried with the mummified body, the paintings were expected to "come to life" and take care of the deceased in the next world.

Materials you will need:
A piece of wood or Masonite, a wide, flat brush, plaster of Paris, tempera or acrylic paints, paintbrushes, chalk, terra-cotta colored pencil or pastel, scrap paper the same size as the wood panel, colored tape

1. Choose a scene from your daily life or a historic scene. Make a sketch of it on a piece of scrap paper the same size as the wood or masonite panel. Do not use any perspective in your drawing, but follow the same rules the Egyptian artists used.

2. Brush plaster of Paris over the wood or Masonite as in Figure 1 to create a smooth surface about ⅛ inch (0.3 cm) thick.

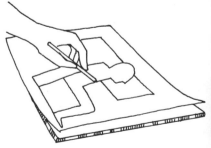

Figure 1

3. When the panel is dry, transfer your sketch onto it using chalk, the terra-cotta colored pencil, or pastel, as in Figure 2.

4. Paint in the areas with flat colors. Do not use any shading.

5. When your painting is finished, frame it or cover the panel edges with a border of colored tape.

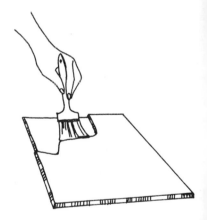

Figure 2

A Jeweled Pectoral

A pectoral is a type of jeweled breastplate or pendant worn on the chest. The ancient Egyptians wore elaborate pieces of jewelry with magical signs or motifs worked into the designs to ornament their bodies and to protect themselves from harm. Often the pectoral was in the shape of Ba, a bird with outspread wings. This symbol represented the Egyptian concept of the human soul. When a person died, and the soul left the body, it was believed to be in the form of Ba. A picture of Ba was often painted on mummy cases or on pieces of decorated furniture buried with the dead. In our example, Ba has a human head, which is a portrait of the young King Tutankhamun, who died at the age of eighteen. The original of this ornament was found in King

Tutankhamun's tomb. His neck is adorned with a typical Egyptian beaded collar called a *wesekh*. The bird's claws hold the hieroglyphic character *shenu*, meaning Universal Power.

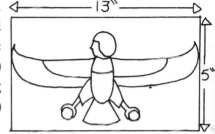

The original of this pectoral was made of gold, inset with pieces of semiprecious stones—turquoise, lapis lazuli, and carnelian. To wear as a breastplate, make the size of the pectoral about 5 inches (12.5 cm) high by 13 inches (33 cm) long. You can also wear it as a piece of jewelry, by reducing the size to about 2¾ inches (7 cm) high by 7 inches (18 cm) long.

Figure 1

Materials you will need:
Stiff gold foil measuring 5 inches × 13 inches (12.5 × 33 cm), pencil, scissors, ruler, glue, permanent black felt-tip pen, tracing and scrap paper, shiny-surfaced paper in turquoise, dark blue, and red or dark red-orange, ribbon

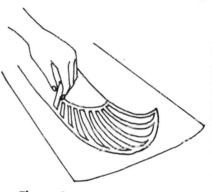

1. Cut scrap paper 5 inches × 13 inches (12.5 × 33 cm). On this paper, draw the basic shape shown in Figure 1. Use tracing paper to transfer the design to the gold foil. You can simply tape your sketch over the foil and draw over it, while pressing down with the pencil, to mark the lines in the foil below.

Figure 2

2. Cut narrow strips of colored paper following the design shown, or make a feather pattern of inlaid strips using the three colors. The colored strips should be glued down side by side leaving narrow bands of gold showing around and between them, as if the colored pieces were separated by narrow pieces of gold wire, as in Figure 2.

3. Use the black felt-tip pen to draw in the facial features and the black hair, as in Figure 3.

4. If you have made the smaller design, make a small hole in the head and string a ribbon through it.

Figure 3

Queen's Headdress

Although dress varied from period to period, the Egyptians wore light, loose clothing mostly made from linen. Most clothing was white, but colors were also used. Men wore kilts of different lengths. Sometimes the wealthy wore cloaks over their kilts. Peasants and slave women wore short skirts. Most women wore a simple tunic with two shoulder straps. On special occasions, they wore fancy over-dresses, sometimes decorated with beadwork or feathers. Young children usually went naked.

Both men and women wore makeup and perfume. They were fond of jewelry and wore rings, necklaces, bracelets, and hair ornaments made from hammered gold. Men and women carefully styled their hair. Upper class Egyptians wore elaborate wigs and headdresses, and royalty wore crowns.

Materials you will need:
Strips of fabric, needle and thread or stapler, scissors, pencil, heavy-duty aluminum foil, enamel paints or oil-base felt-tip pens

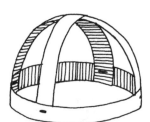

Figure 1

1. Measure around your head, just above the ears. Add 2 inches (5 cm) to this measurement to allow for the fastening.

2. Cut a strip of material 1½ inches (3.75 cm) wide by 23 inches (57.5 cm) long. Wrap it around your head to fit snugly. Sew or staple the ends together.

3. Cut two strips of material ½ inch (1.25 cm) wide by 12 inches (30 cm) long. Staple or sew the ends of these strips to the hatband, making a cross as shown in Figure 1. Try the cap on for fit; it should be comfortable.

Figure 2

4. Cut two 16-inch (40-cm) squares of aluminum foil. Set the cap upside down on the two layers of foil and wrap the cap with the foil. Cover the bands with it as shown in Figure 2. While supporting the cap inside and outside with your hands, press the foil over the crossed strips.

5. Using enamel or oil-base felt pens, paint the cap with the feather design shown, as in Figure 6.

6. To make the bird's head, cut a piece of foil 1½ inches (3.75 cm) by 5½ inches (13.75 cm). Draw a dotted line 1 inch (2.5 cm) up from the end, and another line 2 inches (5 cm) further along from that. Draw and shape the head and pointed beak in the remaining 2½ inches (6.25 cm) as shown in Figure 3. Cut out, tapering the width of the neck down, as shown.

7. Draw the tail shape as shown in Figure 4 on a piece of foil 4½ inches (11.25 cm) square. Decorate the front and back of the tail in the feather design.

8. Cut it out and fold the bottom under 1 inch (2.5 cm) as shown in Figure 5. Fit the fold into the middle of the back of the cap and sew or staple it on.

9. Draw eyes on the bird. Fold it as shown, and attach the bird to the front of the hat.

10. To make the wings, cut the foil or fabric 6 inches (15 cm) × 20 inches (50 cm). Cut the wings in a curve as shown in Figure 6. Decorate with feather designs. Sew the wings on, making sure that they hang down equally on each side of the headdress.

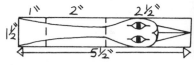

Figure 3

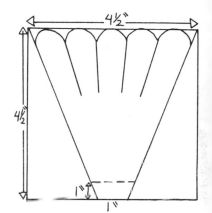

Figure 4

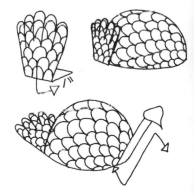

Figure 5

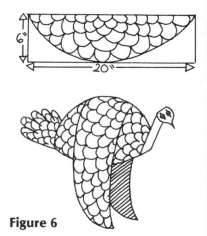

Figure 6

King's Crown

Materials you will need:
Heavy-duty aluminum foil, tape measure, scissors, tape or stapler, pencil

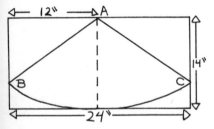

Figure 1

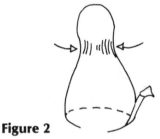

Figure 2

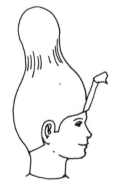

Figure 3

1. To make the basic shape, cut a piece of foil 14 inches (35 cm) wide by 24 inches (61 cm) long. Mark the midpoint A as shown in Figure 1 and mark the side points B and C 14 inches (35 cm) from midpoint A. Connect the three points, and draw a curved line from B to C.

2. Cut out the shape drawn. Pull the ends together and tape or staple the bottom edges so that the cone fits around your head. To make the rounded top, put one hand inside the cone and squeeze in the top third gently (Figure 2).

3. Make and attach a bird's head (see Queen's headdress) to the front of the crown. You can spray paint the entire crown if you want to.

4. Cut out the ear area on the crown as shown, so that you can wear the crown lower on your head, as the Egyptians did (see Figure 3).

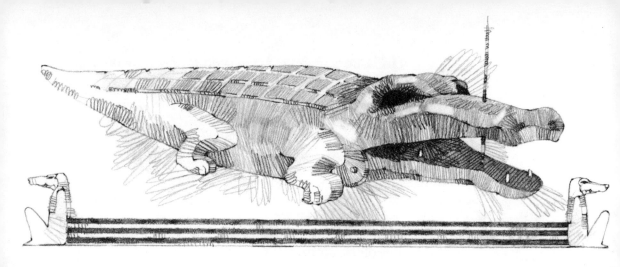

A Movable Crocodile

The Egyptians worshiped many gods and goddesses. Some of these deities were represented by animals or birds. At other times, human bodies were shown with the heads of animals or birds, so that the god represented would be easily recognized. When someone died, statues of the various gods needed to protect that person in the next life were placed in the tomb. Many of the small statues that have been discovered are funerary objects of this type. Other small statues, often in the forms of the animal gods, were made as toys for young children.

The Egyptians made movable toys, often in the form of animals with hinged jaws that could be raised and lowered by pulling a string. One such figure, a wooden crocodile with a movable jaw, is the model for our statue. It probably dates from 1100 B.C., and is now in the Egyptian Museum in East Berlin.

Petesuchos was the name of the sacred crocodile belonging to or symbolizing the god Suchos, also called Sebek. Petesuchos was thought to incarnate the soul of Sebek, the great god of the province of Faiyum. Sebek's chief sanctuary was in Crocodilopolis, the capital of the province.

The Egyptians cared for and worshiped sacred animals to a degree which is amazing to the modern mind. Whole crocodile cemeteries have been found showing fully mummified crocodiles buried with their newborn and even with their eggs.

Materials you will need:
Self-hardening clay, modeling tools, ruler, string, darning needle or narrow nail about 2 inches (5 cm) long, thin string or wool, candle wax (to melt on end of string to stiffen it, if not threading wool through needle), toothpicks or pieces of wood

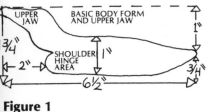

Figure 1

1. Model the basic body form from clay as shown in Figure 1. The crocodile can be any size you wish, from very large to the small model size shown. Our model is 6½ inches (16.25 cm) long and 1¾ inches (4.3 cm) high. Follow these basic measurements, or enlarge them if you wish, keeping the body measurements in proportion. Note especially the modeling of the shoulders. They are slightly rounded, about ⅜ inch (1 cm) thick, and are the points where the lower jaw hinges.

2. Form the inside of the upper jaw. Note that the bottom area is curved inward between the two forward curving shoulder-hinge areas (see Figure 2).

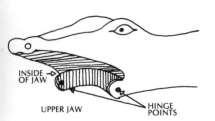

Figure 2

3. Model the lower jaw 2 inches (5 cm) long and ½ inch (1.25 cm) thick at the base. There should be a pronounced lump beneath its front end (see Figure 3).

4. Make teeth by using the broken stubs of toothpicks or other small pegs, or model them out of clay. Put a few in the lower and a few in the upper jaw, as shown in Figure 4.

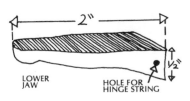

Figure 3

5. Carefully fit the base of the lower jaw inside the shoulder area of the body. Be sure that it fits well. The shoulder hinges of the body should protrude in front of the base of the jaw far enough to run a hinge pin through each shoulder *and* the jaw. (See Figure 4.)

6. Now fit the lower jaw into place. Hold the lower jaw carefully in position between the shoulders and poke the darning needle through the middle of one shoulder, through the lower jaw base, and out the other shoulder. Remove the needle.

7. Still holding the jaw in position, make holes for the lift string through the upper and lower jaws. These holes should be in a straight line about ¾ inch (2 cm) in from the front end of the nose (see Figure 4).

8. Set the lower jaw aside until the clay is thoroughly dry. Occasionally check the holes. If they look closed, open them gently with the needle, but do not alter the jaw's form.

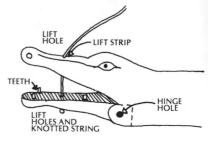

Figure 4

9. Complete the modeling of the body by shaping the eyes, making a crossed-line pattern along the back, and by adding two legs on each side, as shown in Figure 5. Be careful during handling not to alter the form of the head and shoulder area, especially where there are needle holes.

10. Set the body aside until the clay is thoroughly dry. Sand away any rough spots. Paint the body or leave it natural.

11. Fit the lower jaw in place. If the jaw is too tight, sand or file it smaller until it fits between shoulders and the holes line up.

12. Thread a needle with thin string or wool, or drip wax on the string end to stiffen it. Poke the string or needle through the hinge holes and out the other side. Knot the string as close to the shoulder as possible. Cut off any excess string.

13. Repeat the string process to place the pull string through both jaws (see Figure 4). Knot the string under the lower jaw, but leave the pull string long enough above the upper jaw. Pull the string to move the jaw up or down.

Figure 5

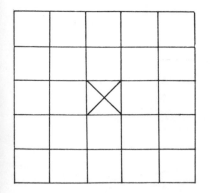

Senat: An Ancient Board Game

Senat is based on a board game that was popular in ancient Egypt. Pictures of Senat players have been found in tomb paintings from the pyramids. They portray players seated on the floor playing Senat on a board raised on a table.

Senat is similar to our game of checkers. It is played on a square board with an uneven number of squares, usually 25. The squares are called "oyoon," meaning eyes. There are the same number of squares across the length and the width of the board, five or a larger uneven number.

The two players each have 12 pieces called "kelbs." The object is to capture the opponent's kelb by coming up alongside it and trapping it with your own kelb on each side. In this case, you take the kelb off the board. The player with the highest number of his or her opponent's kelbs wins.

Materials you will need:
Cardboard, ruler, 12 checkers, stones, or marbles of one color, 12 checkers, stones, or marbles of another color, dice

Making the Board:
1. On a piece of cardboard or heavy paper draw a large square. Divide the square into smaller squares five across and five down. There will be 25 squares in all.

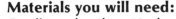

Figure 1
The plain board

2. Each player has 12 pieces of one identifying color or shape. There are 24 kelbs in all. (See Figure 1.)

Placing the Pieces:

1. Roll the dice or throw out your fingers to see who goes first.

2. The game begins by placing the kelbs. To do this, the first player sets out two kelbs in any two squares except the central eye. This *must* remain empty. There is an advantage to placing your kelbs on the outside edge.

3. The second player sets out two kelbs in any two squares except the central eye. Repeat until all the kelbs are set out. Fill up all eyes but the central one on the board. (See Figure 2.)

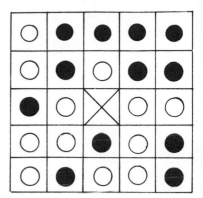

Figure 2
Board with all pieces placed

Playing the Game:

1. After all the kelbs are on the board, roll dice or throw fingers again to see who goes first.

2. Kelbs can move forward, backward, and sideways but not diagonally. Kelbs *cannot* jump over other kelbs. In one turn, a player can move only one kelb one space. At first, the board is crowded and there are few moves you can choose. On the first move, one player must move into the center square. (See Figure 3.)

3. As the board clears, the game grows more complex. If you are blocked on all sides by kelbs and cannot move, you forfeit your turn. The opponent must, however, in his or her next turn, open up a space for you to move into.

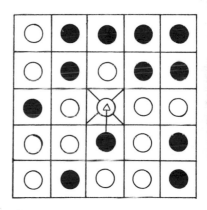

Figure 3
A typical opening move

4. A kelb can be taken only if your opponent comes up alongside you and traps you between two of his or her kelbs. If you *voluntarily* put your own kelb between two of your opponent's kelbs, your kelb *cannot* be taken.

5. If you capture a kelb, you can take another turn, only if in that next turn you can capture another kelb. Repeat this as long as it is possible.

6. A player loses when he or she cannot move the kelbs any further or when he or she refuses to move, or when he or she has had all or most of the kelbs taken. (See Figure 4.)

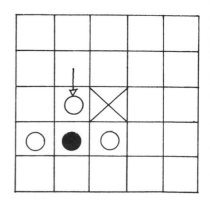

Figure 4
The end of the game

The Chariot:
A War Machine

The chariot was a vehicle that revolutionized warfare, for the army's speed no longer depended solely on the pace of marching foot soldiers. New tactics and methods of warfare resulted.

The Egyptians learned to make chariots from the Hyksos people, an Asiatic tribe that invaded Egypt in 1786 B.C. The earliest chariots were lightly constructed and easy to handle. They carried a driver and one or two warriors. The chariot was drawn by a pair of yoked horses controlled by bridle and bit. Two Y-shaped pieces of wood were attached to the yoke to fit over the shoulders of the horses. The earliest chariots had wheels with only four spokes, which limited the type of terrain over which they could travel.

Chariots have been found in Egyptian tombs that show the craftsmanship of the period. The wheelwright was a

highly skilled worker. Woods of varying properties of hardness and flexibility were used for different parts of the vehicle.

Materials you will need:
86-inch (218-cm) length of flexible wire such as plastic-coated electrical wire, 6-inch (15-cm) coat hanger wire, wire cutters, paper, cardboard or posterboard, scissors, pencil, ruler, white glue, rubber cement (optional), colored pens or crayons, masking tape or brown cloth tape, pliers, plasticene clay

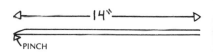

Figure 1

1. To make the chariot body, bend a 28-inch (71-cm) length of flexible wire in half and pinch-fold it with pliers. Be sure the doubled-over wire is straight (see Figure 1).

2. Wrap the doubled-over wire 8 inches (20 cm) from the fold with overlapping twists of tape.

3. Spread apart the remaining 6 inches (15 cm) of each branch of wire into a curve. The ends of the curved wire should be 5 inches (13 cm) apart (see Figure 2).

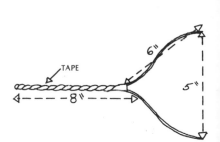

Figure 2

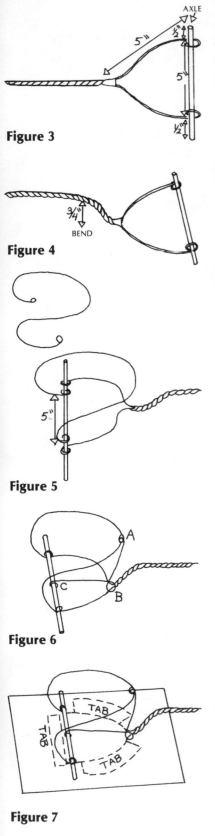

Figure 3

Figure 4

Figure 5

Figure 6

Figure 7

4. Make an axle from a piece of stiff coat hanger wire 6 inches (15 cm) long. Use pliers to pinch and curl the ends of the chariot body wires around the axle, as shown in Figure 3. Keep the space between the wires on the axle 5 inches (13 cm) apart. About ½ inch (1 cm) of the axle should extend beyond each fastening point.

5. Make a slight bend in the taped body pole near the place where the legs split, as shown in Figure 4. The height of the bend is about ¾ inch (2 cm).

6. To make the cage frame of the chariot, cut a 15-inch (38-cm) length of flexible wire and bend it into the curve shown in Figure 5. Use pliers to pinch the ends of the frame wire over the axle. Join them just *inside*, where the pole legs meet the axle. Keep the joints 5 inches (13 cm) apart. The cage curve should be bent to match the curve of the pole legs that it sits above (see Figure 5).

7. Cut a piece of flexible wire 9 inches (23 cm) long. Pinch and curl one end of it to the center top of the cage at Point A, as shown in Figure 6. Bring the other end down and around the pole at the junction of the curved legs (Point B). Then bring it over and wrap the other end around the center of the axle (Point C). If the fastening points slide, tape or glue them.

8. Now make the floor of the chariot. Set the chariot on a piece of paper and draw an outline of the carriage bottom (dotted line, Figure 7). Then draw three tabs as shown, one extending from each side. Cut around the outside of this shape and fold up the tabs.

9. Take a sheet of flexible paper 8½ inches by 11 inches (21.25 × 27.5 cm). Fold it in half, to make a piece that is 8½ inches by 5½ inches (21.25 × 13.75 cm). On this folded sheet, make the front cover of the chariot by copying the diagram shown in Figure 8. Be sure to place the paper fold along the side indicated on the diagram. Draw tabs as shown. With the paper folded, cut out the shape. Do not cut along the fold.

10. Unfold the shape you have cut out. On the front side, draw a woven reed pattern with crayons or pens as shown in Figure 9.

11. Fit the "woven" chariot cover onto the framework with the decorative side facing out. Glue the chariot cover tabs over the wires, pressing the paper onto itself, as shown in Figure 9.

12. To fasten the chariot floor base, fit the base paper (made in step 8) underneath the chariot framework. Glue the tabs of the base up and over the wires at edges.

13. To make the chariot wheels, cut two flexible wires each about 17 inches (42.5 cm) long. Twist the wires into two circles, each about 5 inches (13 cm) in diameter. Wrap the wires with an overlapping band of tape to make them smooth. Cover the twisted ends (see Figure 10).

14. Make the spokes and rims of the wheels from cardboard. Draw two cardboard (or posterboard) circles, each 5 inches (13 cm) in diameter. Make a rim ¼ inch (.6 cm) wide. On each circle make four spokes, drawn where the circle is divided into quarters. (See Figure 11.) The spokes should also be ¼ inch (.6 cm) thick. Cut out the wheels and spokes and glue them flat onto the wire wheel frames.

15. Use small cardboard or metal washers to hold the wheels upright on the axle. If using cardboard, cut four discs ½ inch (1.25 cm) in diameter. Make cone-shaped hubs out of clay or glue as shown in Figure 12. Assemble the wheels, placing a washer on each side of the wheel as it is slipped onto the axle. Poke the axle through the middle of the spokes and washer.

16. To make a yoke similar to the ones the Egyptians used for their chariot horses, follow the diagram shown in Figure 13 and copy it on a piece of cardboard. Cut out the yoke and punch a centerhole through the pointed end of the chariot body pole.

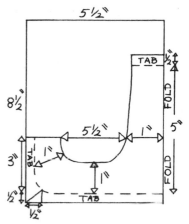
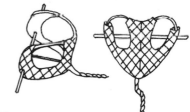

Figure 8

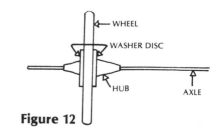

Figure 9

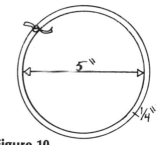

Figure 10

Figure 11

Figure 12

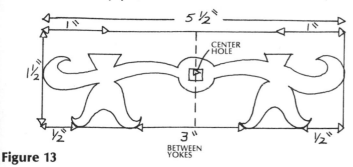

Figure 13

Index

Alexander the Great, 5
Animals, worship of, 23

Ba jewelry shape, 18
Burials, 9–11

Cartouche, 14
Chariots, 28–31
Cleopatra, 5
Clothing, 20
Crocodile, movable, 23–25
Crown, king's, 22

Dynasties, 5

Egypt, 3–5

First Dynasty, 13
Frieze paintings, 16–17

Giza, 6
Great Pyramid of Cheops, 6

Headdress, queen's, 20–21
Hieroglyphics, 12
House of the dead, 6–8
Hyksos people, 28

Jewelry, 18–19

Kelbs, 26

Life after death, belief in, 9
Lower Egypt, 3

Mummification process, 9

Narmer, King, 3
Nile River, 3

Oyoon, 26

Papyrus, 13
Pectoral, jeweled, 18–19
Petesuchos, 23
Pharaohs, 3, 4
Picture writing, 12
Ptolemaic Dynasty, 5
Pyramids, 6

Religion, 4

Sahara Desert, 3
Scribes, 13
Scrolls, 13–14
Sculpture, 4–5
Sebek, 23
Senat (board game), 26–27
Shenu, 19
Statues, funerary, 23
Suchos, 23

Temple paintings, 16–17
Tomb paintings, 16–17
Tutankhamun, King, 18–19

Upper Egypt, 3

Wesekh, 19
Wheelwrights, 28